Making
Cushion Covers

Making
Cushion Covers

Debbie Shore

SEARCH PRESS

First published in Great Britain 2012

Search Press Limited
Wellwood, North Farm Road,
Tunbridge Wells, Kent TN2 3DR

Photographs by Garie Hind

Text copyright © Debbie Shore 2012
Photographs © Garie Hind 2012
Design copyright © Search Press Ltd. 2012

ISBN: 978-1-84448-730-1

The Publishers and author can accept no responsibility
for any consequences arising from the information,
advice or instructions given in this publication.

Suppliers
For details of suppliers, please visit the Search Press
website: www.searchpress.com.

Publisher's note
All the step-by-step photographs in this book
feature the author, Debbie Shore, demonstrating
how to make cushion covers. No models have
been used.

Acknowledgements

Just to Mum, to thank you for instilling in me
a need to save a ridiculous amount of fabric,
buttons and zips, to recycle so much of what
others think of as rubbish, and for teaching me
a skill that I always had but never realised until
you were gone. I've turned into my mother's
daughter, I'm so pleased to say.

Retro mania

Making cushion covers doesn't have to cost the earth. I made this soft and colourful retro-style cushion using an old brown crocheted top left over from the seventies and added a contrasting orange felt lining to add a bit of 'zing'. See page 83 for a similar design.

Contents

Basic envelope cushion, page 22

Basic hand-finished cushion, page 26

Basic Oxford cushion, page 28

Rosette cushion, page 42

Box pleat cushion, page 44

Little box pleats, page 48

Battenburg cushion, page 64

Woven ribbon cushion, page 66

Flower cushion, page 70

Pleated ribbon cushion, page 74

Pleated edge cushion, page 76

Round cushion,
page 30

Corded cushion,
page 34

Two-tone corded cushion,
page 36

Knot cushion,
page 38

Alternative knot design,
page 41

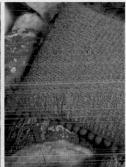

Patchwork cushion,
page 50

Shirring cushion,
page 54

Frilly edged cushion,
page 56

Handkerchief cushion,
page 58

Buttoned cushion,
page 62

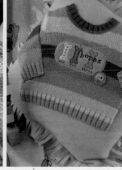

Cardigan cushion,
page 80

Crochet cushion,
page 83

Baby clothes cushion,
page 84

Heart cushion,
page 86

Union Jack cushion,
page 90

About me ...

My name is Debbie Shore. I've had an interest in sewing and recycling since I was a child and have spent years of trial and mainly error learning shortcuts to making professional-looking soft furnishings that I would like to share with you.

My mother taught me how to sew when I was young. We were on a tight budget in the sixties, but my dolls wore my interpretation of couture – hot pants were all the rage in the seventies! By the eighties I had my own home to decorate and the first of my three children to dress.

I've realised over the years that things I find easy to create are difficult for many people, so I've decided to share with you some of my ideas, techniques, hints and tips to help you get creative and start to save money!

Adding a homely touch
A few colourful cushions scattered on a sofa or bed can turn a formal room into a warm and welcoming one.

Introduction

Making cushion covers is one of the easiest ways to brighten up a room, add a touch of luxury and comfort to your living space, and bring colour to your bedroom and decadence to your dining room.

Cushions make a bold statement. When theming a room, blue and white stripes say 'nautical'; flowered fabric is charmingly 'country'; rich velvets are indulgent; red, purple and orange are typically Moroccan.

I'm a big believer in recycling and using up scraps, and like using different techniques to make my cushions unique and fun. Scrap fabric is everywhere — children's old clothes, grown-out-of jeans, pretty dress fabric, unused tablecloths, last year's bedding — simply look around you and you will find a seemingly endless supply!

For most of the cushion covers in this book I've chosen a basic envelope style, which is easy to make as it doesn't involve hand-sewing or zips, but if your cushion cover has detail on both sides, hand-finishing would be better. I don't believe in making hard work where it's not necessary, so I have also included a quick way to fit a zip. Most of the cushion-cover fronts will work with any style of fastening.

I'll show you my way of making cushion covers, though there's no right or wrong way to do it. My aim is to teach you the techniques and inspire you to get creative with fabrics. You will soon become a designer in your own right, adding your own flair and individuality to the covers you create.

I hope you enjoy making the cushion covers in this book, and enjoy the compliments you will receive on your talent and good taste even more!

Useful things ...

A sewing machine: nothing fancy, as we're only using a straight stitch for these projects.

Thread: to match your fabric. Choose the most expensive you can afford as it's usually the best quality, and try to match the fabric content with the thread (cotton with cotton, polyester with polyester, etc.).

Fabric: woven fabric works better as it doesn't twist.

Trimmings: if you're decorating your cushions.

Buttons: you can never have enough buttons!

Scissors: a good-quality pair.

Dressmaking shears: for cutting long lengths of fabric and straight lines.

Pinking shears: to help stop edges fraying or to decorate felt.

Pins: I use glass-headed pins as they don't melt if you pass the iron over them.

An iron: with a clean sole plate!

Tape measure: not a fabric one, as these tend to stretch.

Set square: to make sure your cushions are square.

Tailor's chalk: to draw your stitch line; disappearing pens are also suitable.

Hand-sewing needles

A thimble

Strong fabric glue

Cushion pads: feather pads feel nice if they're on a sofa, but if you're just dressing a bed, hollow fibre is much more affordable.

A quick-unpick or seam ripper: a tool for unpicking those inevitable mistakes and undoing seams.

Kettle: for making a nice cup of tea.

Before you start ...

... read through this section and familiarise yourself with some of the techniques that, though really simple to learn, will give your cushions a neat, professional finish.

Tacking/basting

This is just to keep fabrics in place before machining, so the colour and evenness of the stitches doesn't matter – they won't be seen. Unpick after machining if you can see the stitches, otherwise leave them in.

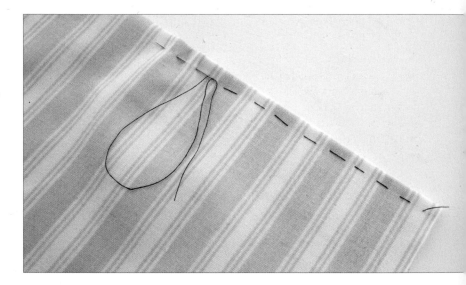

Slip stitch

Use this for fabrics that overlap and for hemming. Try to catch as little of the fabric in the needle as possible on the right side so that it's unlikely you see the stitches.

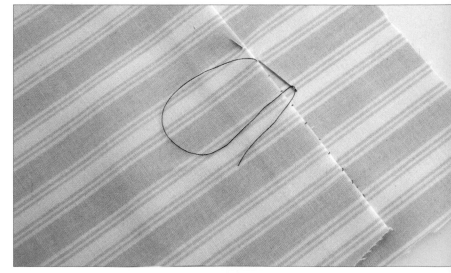

Ladder stitch

This stitch is invisible when done carefully. Use it to join two fabrics that butt together with no overlap. Try to keep the stitches the same length as those made by your machine for a uniform appearance.

Blanket stitch

The heart cushion (page 86) is edged in woollen blanket stitch, but at the opposite extreme a fine blanket stitch can edge a hand-finished buttonhole. Keep the stitches uniform in width and length for the best effect.

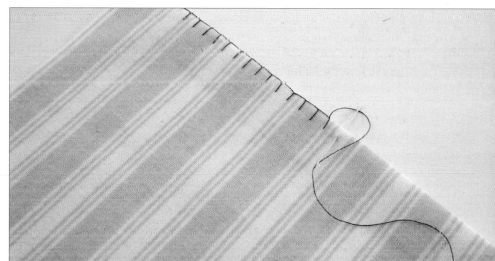

Gathering

I find this easier to do by hand. Use larger stitches on heavy fabric, but try to keep the running stitches a uniform length. The thread won't be seen so it doesn't matter what colour thread you use.

Trimmings

Trimmings really finish off a cushion cover and add a touch of uniqueness to your work. Fringing, cords, tassels or sequins, whatever you choose can make a plain cushion really exciting.

Hand stitch trimmings on to cushions that are used regularly or require washing; stitching lasts longer than fabric glue, but there's nothing wrong with using strong fabric glue if you find it easier.

The daisies in the picture below were snipped off a length of trim and dotted around the cushion. You could be clever here by covering any mistakes in stitching or marks on your fabric by gluing a daisy over them!

Buttons

Buttons can do much more than simply fasten an opening. Using them is a pretty, fashionable and affordable way to embellish your cushions. I inherited jars of buttons from my mum, who used to cut them from clothing before it was recycled (along with zips, hooks and eyes and press studs) and save them for the next dress or skirt!

Buttons can be used to:

accent the corner of a square

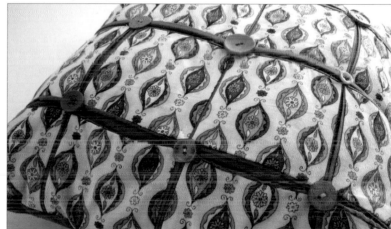

add the finishing touch to a cushion

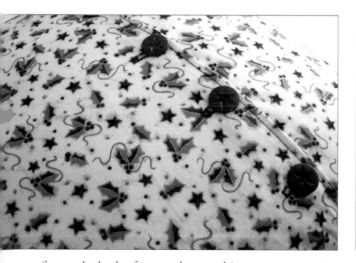

fasten the back of an envelope cushion

finish off the centre of a rosette

Quick zip

If you'll need to remove your cushion cover to wash it, you can either make an envelope cushion (see page 22) or add a zip. This is a quick way to put in a zip — why make life hard?

1 When measuring the back of the cushion cover, add an extra 4cm (1½in) to the width (this includes the seam allowance).

2 Cut the piece of fabric for the cushion cover back in half along its length.

3 Sew the two pieces together again leaving a seam allowance of 2cm (¾in) using your longest straight stitch.

4 Press the seam open.

5 Place your zip along the seam with the teeth on top of the stitching. The zip should be slightly less than the length of your cushion to allow for seams. Pin it in place and baste.

6 Put the zipper foot on your sewing machine and sew along the zip tape on both sides. Remove the basting.

7 Turn the fabric over and, using a seam ripper, carefully snip the stitches to reveal the zip.

Tip

Try and find a zip the same colour as your fabric and it won't be so visible.

The Cushions

Whether making cushions for comfort or decoration, I've tried to keep the techniques as simple as possible. Most of the cushions in this book can be adapted to either an envelope (page 22) or a hand-finished style (page 26), though with some projects I've recommend the style I think works best. Feel free to add a zip if you wish to (page 18).

Basic envelope cushion

This is probably the cushion cover you'll make most often. It doesn't involve zips, and can be removed for washing. This basic cushion cover can be used for most of the projects in this book. Keep it plain or add a decorative trim, contrasting fabrics and textures, and have fun with it!

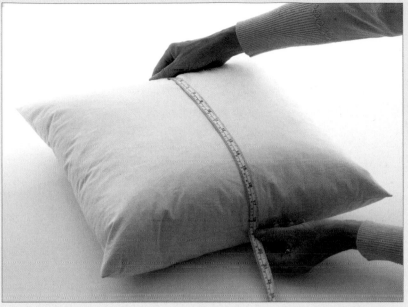

1 Measure your cushion's width and length (for a square cushion these two measurements will be the same). For a well-stuffed look, use these measurements to make the cover; for a looser effect add 2cm (¾in) to each one. In both cases, you will need to add a 1.5cm (⅝in) seam allowance as well.

2 Transfer the length measurement to your fabric along the selvage, as this is a guaranteed straight line.

Tip

To centralise a pattern on your cushion, make a template from tracing or greaseproof paper and place this over your pattern before marking with chalk and cutting out.

3 For the width, use a set square to ensure right-angled corners. Don't rely on the printed pattern as a guideline as it can't be guaranteed to be straight. If your fabric has a woven stripe or check, use this as your guide. Cut out one rectangle. This is your cushion front.

4 For the back, you will need two rectangles, both the same size. One side of each rectangle should measure the same as the width of the cushion front, the other should be about three-quarters the length.

Tip

If you're making cushions to sit on outside, use plastic-coated fabric (the type used for plastic tablecloths) on the back so they don't get damp.

5 Double hem one of the two longest sides of each rectangle. Place both rectangles on the cushion front, right sides together, so that the hemmed sides overlap. Pin the rectangles in place.

6 If you're not confident about sewing straight, use chalk to mark a seam allowance of 1.5cm (⅝in) on all sides. Sew using a medium length straight stitch.

7 Snip across the corners to give a neat finish and press.

8 Turn the cover right side out (this is called 'bagging out') and stuff with a cushion pad.

Tip

To make a feature of the fastening, attach a few ribbons evenly over the envelope opening, either by hand or using a sewing machine, and tie them in bows.

Basic hand-finished cushion

If you have a pattern on both sides of your cushion cover you may not want the opening to be visible. This is an easy alternative, but be aware that if you need to launder the cushion you'll have to unpick the stitches! The alternative is to include a zip – simple instructions for how to do this are on page 18.

I Measure the length and width of your cushion pad, as shown on page 23. Add 3cm (1¼in), 1.5cm (⅝in) top and bottom, to each measurement for the seam allowance; for a well-stuffed cushion, no seam allowance is needed.

2 Cut out two rectangles of this size, using your set square to ensure right-angled corners.

3 Lay the rectangles one on top of the other, right sides facing, and pin. Start sewing with a narrow straight stitch, from 20cm (7¾in) before a corner to around 20cm (7¾in) beyond the last corner, leaving an opening in to which you can stuff your cushion.

4 Press across the open seam with an iron to give you a crease line to hand-sew along.

5 Snip across the corners to ensure sharp corners on turning, and turn right side out.

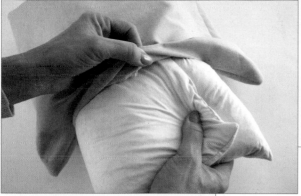

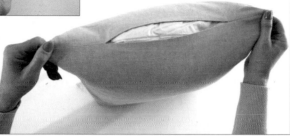

Tip

Roll the cushion as tight as you can to stuff it into the cover, then make sure each corner of the cushion is pushed well into a corner of the cover before you hand-sew together.

6 Insert the cushion into the cover.

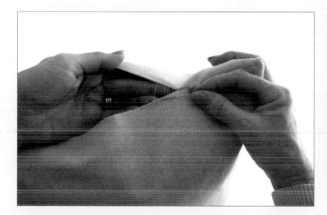

7 Use ladder stitch to carefully sew together the open seam by hand. Keep your ladder stitch as small as you can so that the hand-stitched section looks no different from the machined edges.

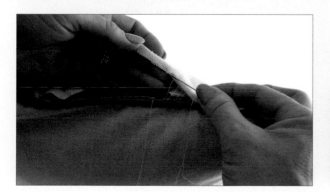

8 If you are hand-finishing a piped cushion cover, apply the piping all the way around one side of the cushion cover after step 6, then continue with step 7.

Basic Oxford cushion

This is a bit of a cheat's way, but why make life more difficult than you need to? A flange creates a border around your cushion that makes it look bigger and more expensive.

1 Measure out the fabric as for the basic envelope cushion (see page 22), but add an extra 11.5cm (4½in) to all four sides, front and back (this includes a seam allowance).

2 Now follow steps 5–8 of the basic envelope cushion (see page 25).

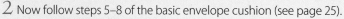

3 Measure 10cm (4in) in from each edge of the cushion cover and mark lightly with chalk or pencil, then sew over this line with a medium straight stitch.

Tip

Don't make the flange too wide as it won't hold its shape when stuffed with the cushion pad, and don't overstuff the cushion cover as this can, again, distort the shape.

4 Press again and insert your cushion.

5 Sew or glue ribbon over the stitch line to add that finishing touch ...

Round cushion

Add different shapes and textures to a cushion arrangement, for example on a bed, for a hint of luxury. This simple round cushion cover will make you look like an expert!

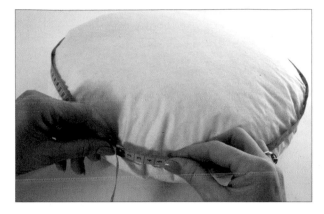

1 Measure the circumference of your cushion pad and add a 3cm (1¼in) seam allowance. This will be the length of your fabric.

2 Squash the cushion pad and measure across the diameter of the pad, adding 4cm (1½in). This will be the width of your cover. You will now have a long rectangular shape.

Tip

A striped fabric makes a striking 'candy lolly' look; large patterns can get a bit lost in the folds, but a plain fabric can look really luxurious. I tried this technique with velvet but the fabric was too heavy to gather and I was left with a large hole in the centre. Fine fabrics work better!

3 Sew together the two shorter sides right sides together, 1.5cm (⅝in) from the edge, to form a tube. Press open the seam.

4 Fold over the two raw edges 1cm (½in) then 1cm (½in) again to make a hem, and stitch as close to the fold as possible as you will be threading cord through this hemline later.

5 Using a quick-unpick, carefully make an opening on the inside of each hem, about 0.5cm (⅛in) long.

6 Take a length of cord or ribbon (you won't see this so the colour doesn't matter) and attach a safety pin to one end. Thread the cord through one hem, then repeat for the other hem.

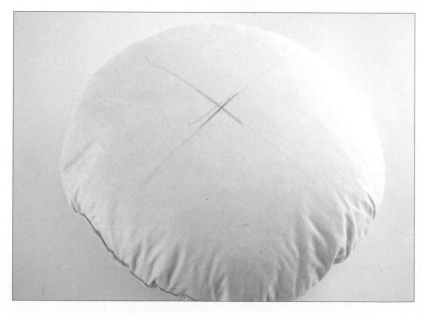

7 Mark the centre of your cushion pad on each side using a pen so that the mark is clearly visible and won't fade.

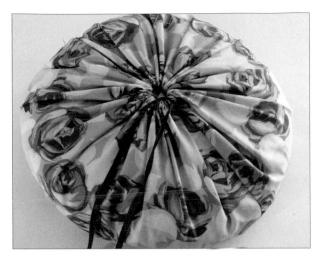

8 Push your cushion pad horizontally through the centre of the tube. Draw up the cord on each side, making sure the gathering sits in the centre of the cushion pad.

9 Tie the cord tightly in a knot, trim the ends and tuck any excess into the hole in the centre.

10 Take two buttons that are large enough to cover the gathers in the centre of the cushion. Secure a strong thread with a large needle in the centre of the gathers, push the needle straight through the centre of the pad and pull it out on the other side. Thread on the first button, then push the needle back through to the other side. Thread on the second button. Go backwards and forwards through the cushion pad and buttons until they feel secure, and tie off your thread so that it doesn't come undone!

Tip

Covered buttons look good in the centre, or you can use a coordinating ribbon and simply tie this in a bow. Pop a dot of glue just underneath it to secure.

Corded cushion

A cord edging gives a professional finish to your projects. Although a wide variety of bias binding is available to buy, it's easy and cost-effective to make your own.

1 Cut out the fabric for your cushion cover following the basic envelope design (see page 22), though any type of cushion can be edged in this way.

2 Measure the perimeter of your cushion. Cut this amount of cord plus about 8cm (3¼in).

3 Using either the same fabric as your cushion or a coordinating fabric, cut the same length in a width of about 4cm (1½in) to make the decorative edging.

(see page 22)

Tip

If you're sewing a rectangular cushion it's fine to cut the edging fabric along the grain, but for curved seams you'll need to cut the strip on the diagonal so it will bend without puckering. If you don't have enough fabric for cutting on the bias, you can buy bias binding from fabric stores that is already cut to width. Bias-cut fabric won't fray and so doesn't need hemming.

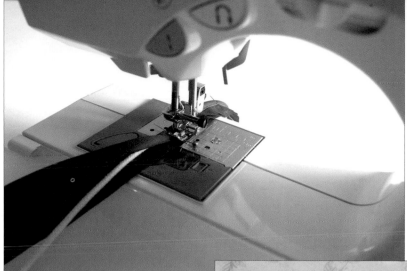

4 Wrap your strip of fabric around the cord and pin it if you wish. Using the zipper foot on your sewing machine, stitch as close to the cord as you can with a long straight stitch.

Tip

You can always go over your stitching again if you're not close enough to the cord.

5 Take your fabric pieces and place them right sides together. Place the covered cord in-between, about half way along one edge, raw edges facing out, and pin all the way around. As you come to the corners it may be easier to snip into the binding, but be careful not to cut through your stitching.

6 When you've pinned the piping all the way around, overlap the two ends by about 6cm (2½in) and neatly pull them out of the way. Be careful as you sew over this join as it will be bulky.

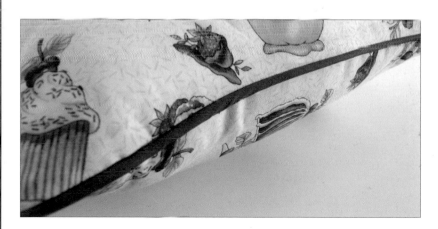

7 Sew, again as close to the cord as you can, using a small straight stitch, making sure you stay tight on the corners. Snip the corners, turn and insert the cushion pad.

Two-tone corded cushion

I initially designed this cushion cover to match a pair of curtains I was commissioned to make, where the top section contrasted with the bottom section. This design also works well with a plain and either a textured or self-striped fabric of the same colour.

1 Cut out the fabric for your cushion back. For the front, take away approximately one-third from the length and cut out the remaining two-thirds from the same fabric.

2 Cut the other one-third from a contrasting fabric, remembering to add a 2cm (¾in) seam allowance.

Tip

This cushion works as either an envelope or a hand-finished design. Instead of using cord, try adding a matching or contrasting trim. Either sew or use fabric glue to attach it to the seam before making up. Fringing or pompoms also look good. Make your own fringe by measuring a rectangle of felt the width of your cushion by about 20cm (7¾in), mark a line with chalk about 2cm (¾in) from the long edge, then snip carefully up to this line with scissors at 0.5cm (⅛in) intervals. This only works with fabric that doesn't fray!

3 Make a strip of cording that is the width of the cushion (see page 35).

4 Join both sections of the cushion front together, sandwiching the cording in between (see page 35).

5 Sew the front and back of the cushion cover together, snip the corners, turn right side out and stuff!

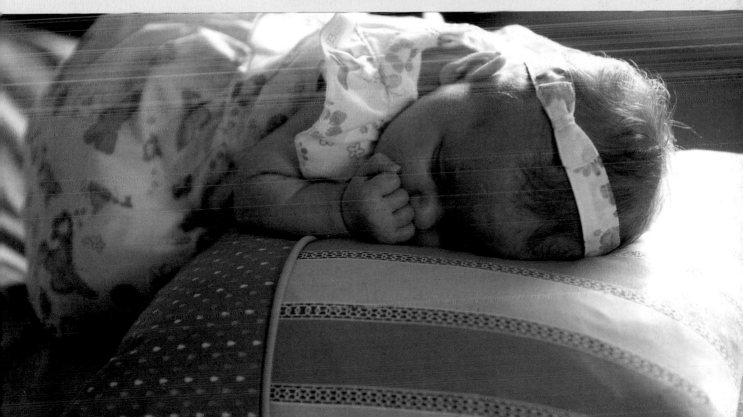

Knot cushion

This is an impressive cushion cover! A little time-consuming, but it looks as though you've spent a fortune in a department store. Satin really shows off the folds as it reflects light, but if it frays it can be difficult to work with. I think fabric with a subtle pattern works most effectively for this design.

1 Measure the front of a square cushion pad, add on a seam allowance of 1.5cm (⅝in) and cut out the fabric for the front and the back.

2 Mark with chalk a point 20cm (7¾in) from each corner, then mark the centre of your square on the right side of the fabric.

3 Measure your square of fabric diagonally and add about 20cm (7¾in). Cut two more pieces of fabric using this measurement for the length and 50cm (19¾in) wide. Run a fine hem along the longer sides.

4 Scrunch each long piece of fabric lengthwise and pin the ends, or for a more structured look you could pleat it, pressing as you go, and pinning the pleats in place.

5 Place your two long pieces on a flat surface to form a cross.

6 Fold each piece in half lengthwise so that they wrap round each other.

Tip

If you use a heavy fabric the knot may be a little bulky, so just use one length of fabric measuring slightly longer than the diagonal, scrunch and pin.

7 Trying to keep this shape, transfer your cross, face up, to the right side of your cover front. Place the centre of the cross in the centre of the cushion using the chalk marks made in step 1.

8 Starting at the corners, pin the ends of the pleats or folds of the cross to the cover, covering the spaces between the corners and your chalk marks. Keep the cross tight but without pulling at the cover fabric. There will be quite a lot of excess fabric at the ends of the cross, but don't worry – you'll trim this later.

9 When you are happy with the arrangement, tack then sew around the raw edge and trim off the excess.

Tip

It may help to place a few hand stitches from the back through to the centre of the knot to keep it in place.

10 Make up the cushion cover, depending on the style of closure you have chosen, then sit back and admire your work!

Alternative knot design

There's no rule to say you couldn't use a contrasting colour for the knot! In this example, I pleated the knot instead of gathering the fabric, and placed the decoration side to side instead of diagonally.

Rosette cushion

This cushion cover was actually made from an old sheet! If you buy new bed linen, buy two sets and make matching cushions. Make sure the fabric isn't too 'floppy' as the rosette needs to have a good shape. And who's to say that you only use one rosette? You could cover the whole cushion cover in smaller rosettes!

1 Cut out both sides of the cushion cover, but don't sew them together yet.

2 Cut a long strip of fabric measuring about 2m (80in) by 20cm (7¾in). Use pinking shears so that it doesn't fray.

3 Fold this strip in half lengthways and press.

Tip

If you find your stitches break when gathering, sew a running stitch by hand instead, and use double thread to make it stronger.

4 Make two rows of long straight stitches along the cut side, 1cm (½in) from the raw edge and 1cm (½in) apart. Before stitching, pull out a long length of thread from the bobbin so that you can identify it afterwards. When you stitch, this will be the bottom thread.

5 Pull gently at the bobbin thread (you'll find it the easier of the two threads to gather).

6 Very gently gather the whole of the length of fabric. It will start to curl.

7 Decide where on your cushion front the rosette looks best. I placed mine in one corner but you may prefer it in the middle. Swirl the gathered panel around, starting from the outside, making sure you can't see the gathering stitches.

8 When you are happy with the rosette, pin it in place, then tack all the way around.

9 Follow the tacking stitch with your sewing machine, using large straight stitches, and simply fold over the centre to neaten. You could even sew a button or bead in the centre to finish off.

10 Sew on the back of the cushion cover, making sure you tuck in the rosette so the stitches don't catch.

Tip

Another idea is to position your rosette in the centre of the cushion cover and sew the whole cover together, then insert your pad and hand sew the opening. Place a button over the centre and sew all the way through the cushion pulling as tightly as you can.

Box pleat cushion

A striking effect for a cushion cover when used with contrasting fabric, this project looks complicated but is quite easy to make. I originally got the idea from a duvet cover, then adapted it for cushions. I chose a patterned fabric for the front panels and a contrasting plain fabric for the pleat – a real show stopper!

1 Measure your cushion front, adding a 2cm (¾in) seam allowance on each side. This gives a 1.5cm (⅝in) seam allowance around the cushion and an extra 0.5cm (⅛in) for the squares.

2 Mark the central line from top to bottom then side to side to divide your fabric into four equal squares. Cut out the squares.

3 Cut two squares of the same size as those in step 2 out of the contrasting fabric, then cut one long piece the size of two squares next to each other.

4 Sew together one patterned square, followed by a plain square, then another patterned square. Do this twice so you have two strips of fabric, each with patterned squares on the outside and one plain square in the middle.

5 Take one strip and mark the centre line of the plain fabric. Fold the patterned pieces over it so that they meet in the middle and the plain fabric is covered. Pin in place with glass-headed pins, then press.

6 Tack then stitch close to the edge over the pleats where you've pinned to hold them in place

7 Repeat with the second strip.

8 Place the two strips together on a flat surface with the pleats going from left to right, and you'll see the design coming together.

9 Now take the plain long strip and place it from top to bottom between the two patterned strips.

10 As with the small pleats, mark the centre, fold in, pin, press and sew in place.

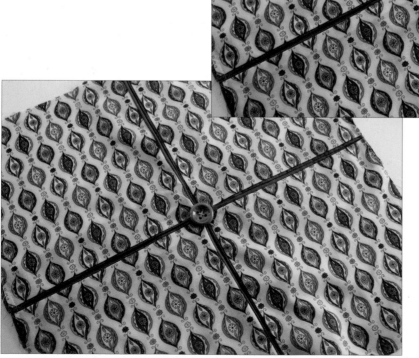

11 Lay the cushion cover flat again and you'll see the 'cross' of plain fabric forming. In the centre, where all four squares meet, pin, then sew an 'x' shape across the join to secure.

12 I like to add a button in the centre to cover the stitches.

13 Sew together with the back of the cushion, snip the corners, turn, press and stuff.

Little box pleats

If you really want to get creative, try this. The instructions are on the next two pages ...

Little box pleats

This is a little more complicated than the previous project, but is well worth the effort!

1 Cut four patterned squares as you did in the previous project. Mark and cut each one of these into four, making 16 squares in total.

2 Cut 12 plain squares and 3 long plain strips that are the width of a square and the length of the cushion.

3 Sew together alternate squares of patterned and plain fabric, starting with patterned, until you have four strips each with four patterned squares separated by three plain squares.

4 Mark the centre of each plain square, fold in, press and sew the edge as in the previous cushion cover.

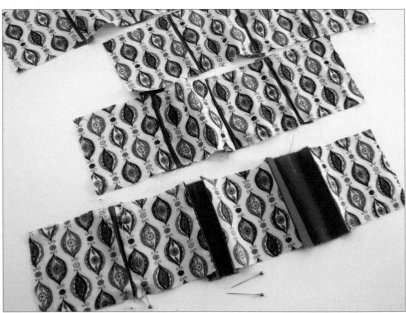

48

5   Join these four strips to the three plain strips and, again, mark the centre of the plain strips, fold in, press and sew over the ends to secure. Don't worry about what the back looks like – it'll be a bit messy!

6   At the joining point of each set of squares, sew an 'x' to hold them in place.

Tip

Just one tip here – be patient!

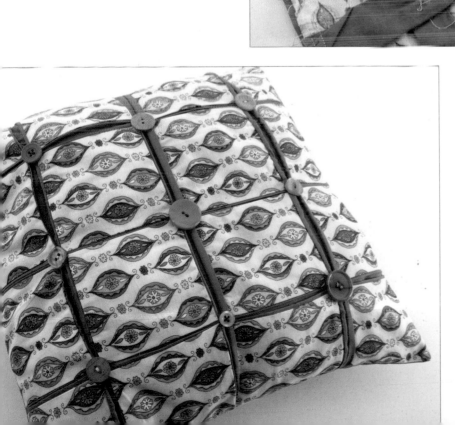

7   I've collected odd buttons over the years and decided to use them up with this cover. You'll need nine buttons to do this.

8   Sew the front together with the back of the cushion cover, snip and press as usual.

Patchwork cushion

Patchwork and quilting have been around for centuries and always have a revival when hard times hit and recycling is necessary. Patchwork is a great way to use up scrap fabric and is so satisfying to complete.

This is a very simple quilted patchwork cover, using only squares and a border. If you're a beginner it's very easy, but if you're a seasoned patchworker you can incorporate your own more intricate designs, and you can get lots of ideas from books, magazines and the internet. A block of 25 squares will cover a cushion of 25.5cm (10in) square, and you could add more squares for a larger cushion. The inch is still the unit used for patchwork; 2½in is about 6.5cm, if that makes more sense to you!

Always use woven fabric that doesn't stretch. Pure cotton is easier to press.

Be imaginative! What about recycling old denim jeans?

1 Making sure you measure accurately, cut twenty-five 6.5cm (2½in) squares of fabric. Choose either bold or gentle prints, not a mixture of the two, so the overall look is even.

2 You'll also need a square of batting and some backing fabric (this could be calico or part of an old sheet), cut to about 2.5cm (1in) larger than the finished patchwork all round to allow for movement when sewing. Cut out the back of the cushion cover according to the type of cushion you are making.

Tip

Have a look on the internet for 'jelly rolls'. These are rolls of coordinating fabrics, about 101.5cm (40in) long and 6.5cm (2½in) wide, specifically designed for patchwork.

3 Sew together the squares into strips of five, chain linking to save on time and thread. Use a small stitch and 0.5cm (⅛in) seam allowance. Press the seams over.

Tip

Chain linking will save you time – and thread. Sew pairs of squares together, moving from one pair to another without snipping the threads. Cut through all the threads at the end.

Tip

If you have light and dark fabrics, press the seams towards the dark so that they don't show through.

4 Sew these strips together to make a square.

5 Make up the size of the cushion by adding a border. Mine is 9cm (3½in) wide. Sew the border to the block, first the top and bottom then the sides. Press. It may be easier to sew the corners by hand.

6 Pin the patchwork to the batting and the backing fabric cut in step 2 using either safety pins or long, flat-headed pins, first in the corners then randomly over the patchwork to hold it in place.

7 Using chalk, draw your quilting design over the front of the patchwork. This could be zig-zag, circles or random 'squiggles'. As an alternative you could just follow the seams around the squares.

8 Using a medium straight stitch and starting in one corner, begin to feed your fabric through and stitch around the inside of the border.

9 Now drop the feed dogs on your sewing machine and, if you have one, attach a quilting foot.

10 Reposition the needle into one corner of the fabric and guide it along your chalk design, making sure you keep the fabric moving.

Tip

Remember that when you've dropped the feed dogs the machine won't pull the fabric through, so try to keep an even pace. If you stop moving, the machine will repeat the stitch on top of itself. Don't worry too much if this happens occasionally; patterned fabric is great for disguising mistakes!

You don't need to turn the fabric to go around curves; you can move it up, down and from side to side when you don't use the feed dogs.

11 When you've finished quilting, trim away the excess batting and backing fabric to 1cm (½in) less than the patchwork front. This is the seam allowance you will need when attaching the back of your cushion cover.

Shirring cushion

Shirring gives a lovely texture to your cushion cover, and works best with plain, fine fabric that gathers well. If you're just shirring the front of your cushion you'll need about three times the size to allow the fabric to 'shrink' when gathered. Some computerised sewing machines won't take shirring elastic, so if the method doesn't work on your machine this may be the reason why.

1 Wind shirring elastic around the bottom bobbin by hand and without stretching it. Although there aren't many colours available, don't worry as the elastic won't be seen. Put regular thread in the top of the machine.

2 Practise the technique on scrap fabric first; you may need to loosen the tension on your machine to get the right effect.

3 With a long straight stitch, sew rows across the fabric, about 1cm (½in) apart. As your fabric starts to gather, take it slowly and smooth the area you're about to sew so that it doesn't pucker.

4 If your panel is too large when finished, cut away the excess.

5 Place right sides together, then sew them together, snip the corners, turn right side out and stuff.

6 I've added some matching pompom trim by hand; ric-rac would work just as well.

Tip

You can create some lovely effects with shirring elastic. Play with a scrap piece of fabric and try sewing in swirls and zig-zags. You don't have to sew all over the fabric — experiment with just a centre section or border.

Frilly edged cushion

Instant girliness! Frills are so feminine and perfect for a little girl's room. I find it easier to hand stitch when gathering as the thread doesn't seem to break so easily, but if you're machining do a double row of your longest stitches. This gives you a safety net in case one thread snaps, but it also makes the gathered fabric lie flatter. It may help to loosen the tension slightly and, when gathering, to pull up the bottom thread.

Tip

You could use wide ribbon as a frill, or choose wide strips of Broderie Anglaise for a 'country' feel. And there's nothing to say this cushion has to be a circle – frills look equally good on heart shapes and squares.

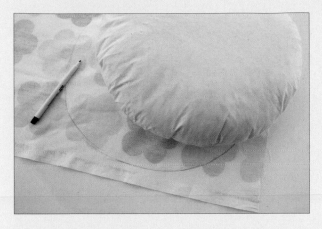

1 I've chosen a round cushion, and am going to hand finish it so that I can use either side. Fold your fabric in half and draw around your cushion pad on the wrong side, then cut 1.5cm (⅝in) outside this edge to accommodate the pad.

2 Cut a strip of fabric about 40cm (15¾in) wide by at least twice the circumference of the cushion. You may need to join a few pieces together. Fold this strip in half lengthways and press. Fold the ends in by about 1cm (½in) and press. Make a running stitch along the raw edge of the folded fabric and gently gather the whole length evenly.

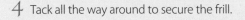

3 Take your cover front and lay it face up, then pin the raw edge of your frill to the cushion edge, so that the frill faces inwards.

4 Tack all the way around to secure the frill.

5 Machine stitch all the way around as close to the edge as you can. Where the ends of your frill meet, tuck one end inside the other and hand stitch them together using slip stitch.

6 Pin to the back of the cushion cover (right sides together) and sew about two-thirds of the way around, making sure your stitch line is inside your gathering line so that you don't see the gathering stitches when you turn it right side out.

7 Stuff the cushion pad into the cover and ladder stitch the opening closed.

Handkerchief cushion

The inspiration for this cushion cover came purely from the fabric. I found this striking monochrome material on the internet and wanted to use as many pieces as possible in one project. The buttons add a touch of fun and the piping gives a clean outline.

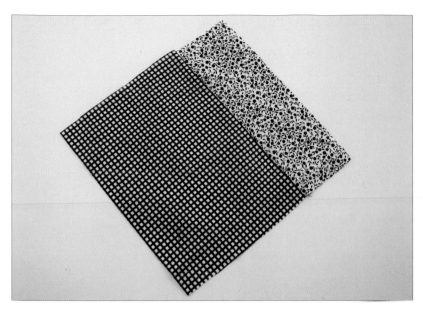

1 Measure your cushion pad and cut out the front and back panels.

2 Cut away about one-third from one end of the front, then make it up using a contrasting fabric. Remember to add a 1cm (½in) seam allowance on the join.

3 Sew the two panels for the front together, then check the measurements again.

4 Cut two 15cm (6in) squares from each of five patterned fabrics, making ten squares all together, and sew each matching pair together on three sides. As though you were making mini cushion covers, snip the corners, turn and hand sew the opening, then press. You'll have five squares.

5 Arrange your squares across the join in the fabrics, and pin them in place when you're happy with the arrangement.

6 Make up the piping as in the corded cushion project (page 35) and sew it around the front of the cushion cover.

7 Fold back the right-hand side of each diamond and machine sew a row of stitches across the left-hand side of the diamond underneath to hold it in place; the stitches will be hidden under the overlapping diamond.

8 Sew on your buttons by hand so that they hold down the right-hand side of each diamond.

9 Fold in the points of the squares that overhang the edge of the cushion cover and pin them out of the way so that they don't get caught when piecing together the back and front panels.

10 Pin the back panel on to the front, baste if you wish and sew together, carefully leaving an opening for stuffing.

11 Snip across the corners, turn right side out and insert your cushion pad. Hand sew up the opening.

Tip

You'll get a very different look to this cushion cover if you use brightly coloured fabrics, and have a play with the 'handkerchiefs'. You may think they look better placed as a row of squares instead of in a diamond design.

Buttoned cushion

This cushion is a variation of the basic envelope design, but instead of the overlap being at the back of the cushion, I've made it into a feature on the front.

   If you don't have a buttonhole foot for your machine, you can make the buttonholes carefully by hand. Draw a line the same size as your button and sew small back stitches all the way around. Carefully cut the hole, then blanket stitch very tightly around it. Or, instead of buttonholes, stitch a one-touch fastening to the closure then just add the buttons to the top. This 'cheat's method' is easy, and stops well-stuffed cushion covers from gaping.

I   When cutting out your envelope cushion shapes, make the two front rectangles narrower than suggested in the basic instructions – they only need to overlap by about 4cm (1½in). Hem one long side of each of the rectangles.

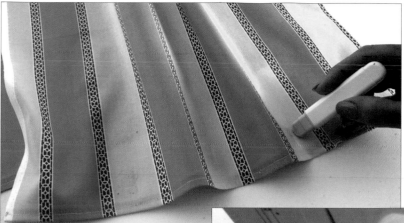

2 Mark at even intervals where your buttonholes should sit, about 1cm (½in) from the hemline.

3 Attach a buttonhole foot to your machine and, using a contrasting coloured thread, sew the buttonholes evenly. Practise this on a piece of scrap fabric first.

4 Snip the buttonhole carefully with a quick-unpick.

Tip

Buttonholes aren't just for buttons – try threading coloured ribbon through the holes instead.

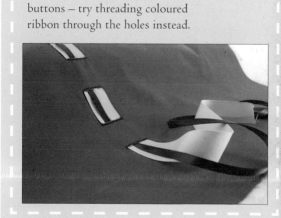

5 Sew together the cushion cover, snip across the corners, turn right-side out and press. Put a pin over the end of the buttonhole before snipping so that you don't cut the stitching.

6 Mark with a pencil the centre of each buttonhole on the fabric underneath and hand sew the buttons over these marks.

Battenburg cushion

This cushion cover can be classy or fun, depending on the colour and texture of the fabrics you choose. Use a colourful cushion to brighten a dull sofa, or to bring together mis-matching colours in a room. This cover works best with a square cushion, and when using the same weight of fabric for each square.

Tip

Instead of using different colours of fabric, cloth with a pile, like velvet, can be used but with the nap facing in the opposite direction for each square. Alternatively, you could cut each one of your four squares into quarters to make a patchwork. Allow for the extra seam allowance if you decide to do this.

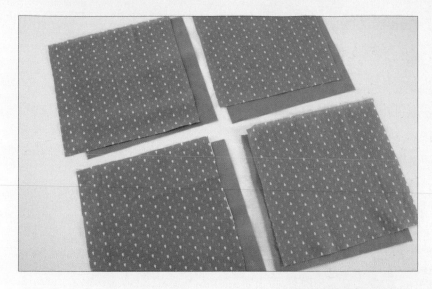

1 Measure the size of your cushion pad then add 2cm (¾in) to each side for a seam allowance. Cut two squares this size, one in each of two contrasting fabrics.

2 Fold each square in half lengthways and cut along the fold, then fold each rectangle in half and cut again. You will now have eight squares.

3 Arrange the squares on a flat surface and swap them around to give a 'Battenburg cake' effect.

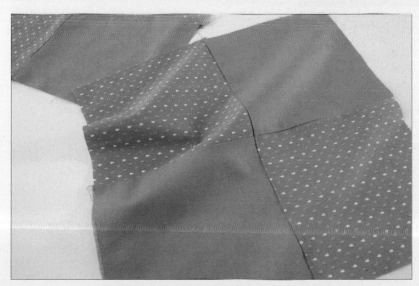

4 Using a small straight stitch, sew together the contrasting squares in twos and press the seams open.

5 Join two of these pieces together, creating your Battenburg look. Repeat for the second panel and press again.

6 Make up the cushion following the instructions for the basic hand-finished cushion (page 26).

Woven ribbon cushion

One nice thing about this cushion cover is that you can use scraps of ribbon in different colours to create a very modern, abstract look; velvets, on the other hand, can look rich and opulent. Easy to make, this is a technique you probably learned at school. The other good thing is the number of people who want to buy these cushions from me!

I   You'll need quite a lot of ribbon – I used about 16m (640in) for my square cushion.

2 First arrange your ribbons in strips so that you are happy with the colour combinations.

3 Cut a piece of backing fabric to the size of your cushion, with a 3cm (1¼in) seam allowance.

4 Pin the ribbon strips across the top of the backing fabric and stitch across the top, about 0.5cm (⅛in) from the edge.

5 Place a pin about halfway down each strip of ribbon to help keep it in place when you start weaving.

6 Now the fun starts! Begin to weave ribbon under and over these strips, again changing the colours to get pleasing colour combinations. If you start the first row 'over', start the second row 'under' to create the woven effect.

Tip

You may find it easier to work if you spray the backing fabric with temporary fabric glue. This helps to hold the ribbon in place when you're weaving. If you're weaving diagonally you'll need to secure the first layer of ribbon on all four sides, and there's no harm in putting the occasional spot of glue under the ribbon to keep in place!

7 Carry on until all the backing fabric is covered, keeping each of the rows tight together without puckering. You can pin as you go along if it helps, but be aware that satin ribbon can mark easily.

8 Pin and stitch around the remaining three sides to secure all the ribbon strips. Finish off your cushion as usual.

Festive spirit

By using glittery gold ribbon, I've created a lovely Christmassy cushion cover. You could even add a little clove or cinnamon to the stuffing to give it a festive fragrance – perfect for cosy nights in front of the fire!

Flower cushion

I saw a similar cushion cover in a department store for £35 – this cover was made for about £5. It is such fun to make – and a good one to get the kids involved in!

I've used felt for this cushion as it doesn't fray, and it would be very fiddly to hem each of the flowers. You can buy really affordable felt by the metre or yard off the internet. I've just used one colour but you could have some fun by creating a whole bouquet in different colours.

Tip

You don't have to cover the whole cushion with flowers, and you could make just one large flower instead. I've used a square cushion in this project, but a rectangular or circular cushion would also work well.

1 Take a side plate or bowl measuring about 30cm (11¾in) across, and a glass or beaker. Use paper to make a pattern. Draw around the plate with a pen, then place the glass just inside the outline and draw around it.

2 Keep going until you have a circle of glass shapes. If they overlap it doesn't matter but they do need to join up. I don't think it matters if the 'petals' aren't uniform in size. Cut out the flower shape.

3 Take your template and draw around it on your felt, this time in chalk, and cut out nine flowers. As felt doesn't fray, you could cut out the flowers using pinking shears or deckle-edged scissors instead.

4 Draw a small circle, using something like a coin, in the centre of each flower. Put a running stitch around this line by hand. Gather up the centre of each flower by pulling on this thread, and your flowers will come to life!

5 Using felt again, cut two squares about 2cm (¾in) larger than the cushion pad. On one of the squares (the cushion front) mark a central line in chalk, then draw one halfway along in each direction to divide your cushion in four. Do the same in the other direction to create a grid.

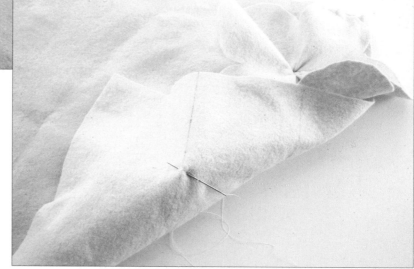

6 From the back, hand stitch each flower to the crossing points of the grid until all nine are sewn on.

7 If you want to add buttons to the centres, now is the time to do it. You could glue on a bead but make sure the glue is dry before sewing the cushion cover together.

Tip

Beads can be expensive – look around for cheap strings of beads in fashion stores or second-hand shops and use these instead.

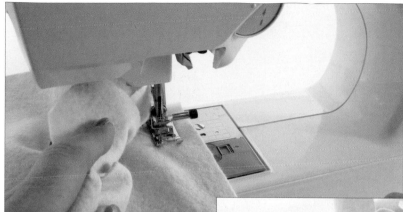

8 Lay the two cushion squares together, wrong sides facing, and sew along three sides.

9 Turn the cushion right side out, stuff in the cushion pad and sew up the remaining side, being careful not to stitch over the flowers.

Tip

You could make a double flower using different-coloured felt – simply cut a second, slightly smaller, flower and stitch the centres together.

Add these flowers to an existing cushion cover to brighten it up!

Pleated ribbon cushion

Pleated ribbons add a wonderful texture to a cushion cover. I got the idea from a similar cushion that I spotted in an interiors magazine, and I managed to cut the cost massively from what they were asking.

I   Cut your front and back panels in the usual way.

Tip

Try rows of different-coloured ribbon for a fun effect, or strips of fabric left raw at the edges to fray, giving a 'shabby chic' look.

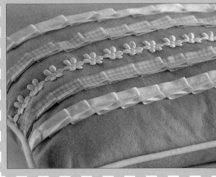

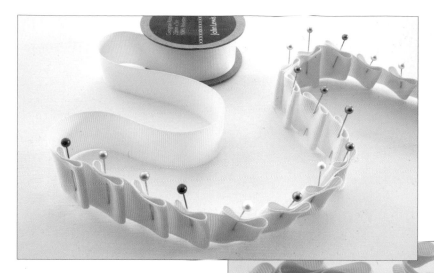

2 You will need around 15 times the width of the cushion cover in ribbon. Begin by pleating the ribbon and pinning each pleat in place. You will need five pleated strips, each measuring the width of the cushion cover.

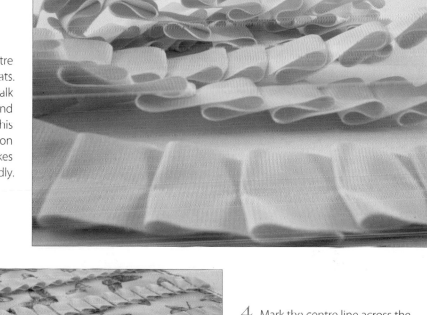

3 Sew straight down the centre of the ribbon to secure the pleats. You could mark this line with chalk if you're not too confident. I find it easier to stitch the pleats at this stage rather than pin directly on to the cushion cover as it makes attaching the ribbon less fiddly.

4 Mark the centre line across the width of your cushion front and pin on the first pleated ribbon. Then measure and pin the other four strips an even distance from each other.

5 With the same colour thread as your ribbon, attach the ribbon using tiny hand stitches. If you are steady, you could machine stitch directly over the centre stitching of the ribbon instead.

6 Make up your cushion cover.

Pleated edge cushion

By putting an edge to a cushion cover you're adding the finishing touch that makes your work look professional. This pleated edge can add that designer touch to a plain cushion cover, and works just as well using a different print but in the same colour as your cushion. If you cut a wider strip of fabric for pleating it will 'flop' a little, which creates a softer look; a narrower strip will keep its crisp edge better.

1 Cut the fabric pieces for your cushion cover. I've made mine using the basic envelope style (page 22).

2 Cut a strip of fabric around 40cm (15¾in) wide by at least three times the perimeter of your cushion. You may need to join a few pieces together for this.

3 Fold the strip in half lengthwise and press. Fold over one end by about 1cm (½in) and press again.

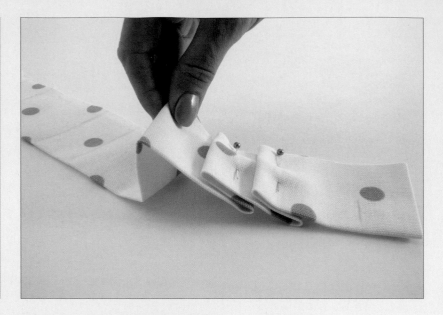

Tip

If you can't get the hang of pleating, you may find it easier to measure and mark with chalk where you should be folding. Draw a line at 3cm (1¼in), then 6cm (2½in) from there, then 3cm (1¼in), then 6cm (2½in) and so on until the whole length is marked. Pinch the 3cm (1¼in) line and fold the 6cm (2½in) line, pin, and repeat all the way along. This isn't as complicated as it sounds, and you'll get into the flow really quickly!

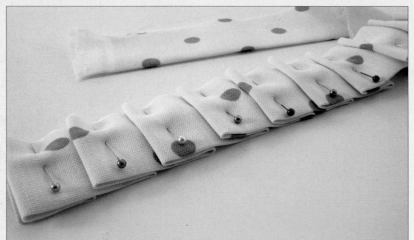

4 Starting at the neat end, pinch the fabric between your fingers, fold over about 3cm (1¼in) and pin. Repeat the folds as evenly as you can, pinning as you go, until the whole length is pleated.

5 Sew as close to the raw edge as you can using a basting or long stitch. Press.

6 Pin the pleats on to the right side of your cushion cover front, with the folded edge of the pleats facing inwards. Try to keep the corners neat; they may feel a little bulky but that's fine.

7 Where the two ends meet, overlap them by a couple of centimetres and trim. Tuck the raw edge inside the pressed edge and pin.

8 Using a long stitch, sew all the way around the trim. Take out the pins.

9 Place the back panels of the cushion cover face to face with the front, pin then sew using a small stitch, making sure this stitch line it slightly within the previous one.

10 Snip the corners and turn. Press again if you need to.

Cardigan cushion

This is one case where it's easier to fit the cushion pad to the cover instead of the other way around, so you don't have to cut more than one side of the cardigan. Button up the cardigan and sew up the opening, then measure across the chest – this is the size of cushion pad you'll need.

I Measure across the chest of the cardigan. Take this measurement from the bottom up to make a square. You should be able to get away with only making one cut just under the arms.

2 With the buttons done up, cut straight across both layers of the cardigan.

Tip

Don't throw away the sleeves – you can use these to cover bolster cushions.

3 Turn the cardigan inside out then hand sew around the bottom edge with a large needle and matching coloured wool, carefully making sure you catch all the cut loops so they don't fray.

4 Turn the cover right side out, insert the cushion pad and sew up the top edge.

5 Cut lengths of wool about 20cm (7¾in) long to make the fringing. You can do this by wrapping the wool around a piece of cardboard 10cm (4in) deep then cutting through the loops at one end.

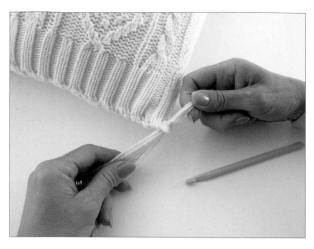

6 Use a crochet hook to pull about four lengths of wool, folded in half, through the corner of the cushion cover.

7 Pull through the loop of yarn ...

8 ... and make a knot.

9 Do this all the way around the cushion at about 2cm (¾in) intervals.

10 Trim any fringing that is longer than the others to even it up.

11 Place the cushion on your sofa and cuddle up!

Crochet cushion

The cardigan cushion works just as well with crochet. This is a little vest top that I cut down to fit my cushion. I used the lining as well so you can't see the cushion pad through the crochet, and added a fringe as with the previous design.

Baby clothes cushion

This design was inspired by my children's baby clothes that I still have, even though they're all grown up now. I think all mums save a favourite dress or pair of jeans, and it's a shame to leave them in a drawer never to be seen again.

This would make a lovely 18th birthday present for the young person who once wore the baby clothes. I've used felt for the cushion cover as it doesn't fray, and is available in some really bright and fun colours.

Tip

It can be fun to cover a cushion cover in dolls' clothes for a child's bed! If a dress is too big for the cushion, you could just use the collar or skirt, or you could take the pocket off a pair of jeans and use that.

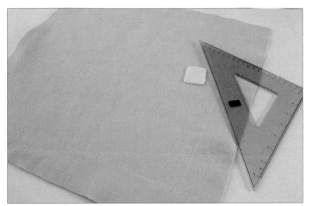

1 Choose your baby garment. If it is too big for your cushion cover, you could fold in the arms or bend the legs.

2 Knitwear is less bulky if you cut off the back. Don't cut away too much; you'll need to tuck the edges in so it doesn't unravel.

3 Measure and cut out your cushion cover, front and back, adding an extra 10cm (4in) for the fringe. Mark this 10cm (4in) border with chalk.

4 Arrange the garment on the fabric at an angle that pleases you, within the chalked border. Mark the position of the garment with chalk.

5 Remove the garment and spray with fabric glue on the wrong side.

6 Re-apply the garment to the fabric. If it is a lightweight fabric you could then sew around the edge of the garment carefully with your sewing machine, but if it's a little bulky it may be easier to sew by hand. I recommend this for knitwear as machine stitching can pull at the knitting whereas hand stitching becomes invisible.

7 Pin both sides of the cushion cover together face up, then sew along your chalk lines on three sides.

8 Stuff your cushion pad into the cover, and carefully sew along the open side with your machine.

9 Now the fun bit – snip the border at 1cm (½in) intervals to make the fringe. Don't cut right it up to your stitch line as you don't want to risk cutting through it.

Heart cushion

What a great Valentines gift! And of course you could change the lettering to spell a name. No machine sewing here – I find it quite relaxing to hand stitch occasionally! You'll need to use felt for this project as it doesn't fray. Try to find quite a heavy-weight felt so that it will keep its shape.

I First, make a template for the heart. You'll need a dinner plate, ruler, pen and a large piece of thin card. Fold the card in half and open it up again.

2 Place the plate about a third of the way over the score line towards the top of the card and draw round it.

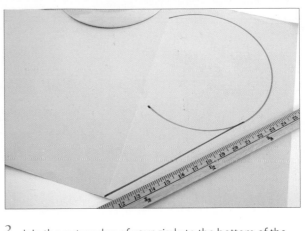

3 Join the outer edge of your circle to the bottom of the score line with the ruler, and mark.

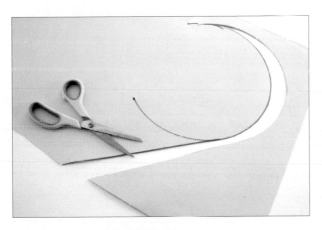

4 Cut around this 'half heart' shape.

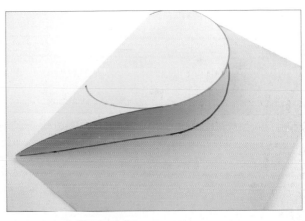

5 Fold in half along the score line, and use the cut-out side as a template to mark the second side of the heart.

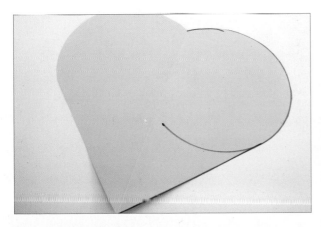

6 Cut out the template.

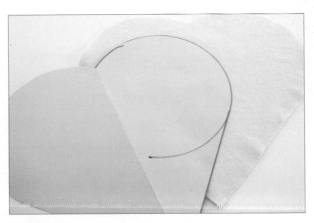

7 Transfer the template to your felt and cut out two hearts.

8 At this point cut out your letters too. Chunky bold letters work best and they don't have to be perfectly shaped – this cushion really suits a home-made look! Begin by writing them on a second piece of card and cutting them out.

9 Use the card letters as templates and cut them out of felt in a colour that contrasts with the cushion.

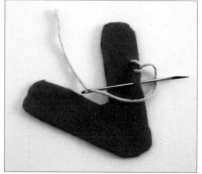

10 With contrasting wool and a large needle, blanket stitch around the edge of each letter.

11 Arrange the letters in place on one of the hearts and, when you're happy with the look, glue them in place with strong fabric glue.

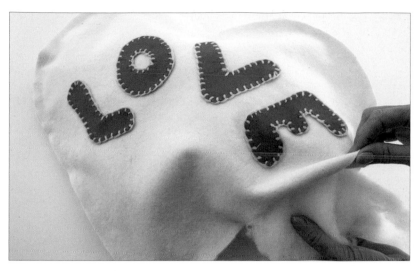

12 Glue around the edge of one heart shape leaving a gap of around 15cm (6in) to insert the stuffing. Put the front and back panels together and leave to dry.

13 When dry, gently stuff the cushion evenly with kapok, being careful not to overfill or your heart will become mis-shapen.

14 Glue together the opening and pin to hold it in place until dry.

Tip

Kapok can be really expensive to buy. Shop around for hollowfibre pillows, which are a fraction of the price, and use the stuffing from those.

15 Blanket stitch around the edge of the heart using yarn in the same colour as the letters. Make sure you start and end the stitching on the back panel, then dot a tiny drop of glue on the end stitch to ensure it doesn't come undone.

Tip

Instead of a plate, draw round a drinking glass or even an egg cup. You will then have a small heart shape that can be used as a pin cushion. Add a sprinkle of dried lavender or pot pourri to the stuffing and pop it in your underwear drawer, or fasten a cord to the top and hang it around a coat hanger for a great and inexpensive gift idea.

Union Jack cushion

I like to use scraps of contrasting fabric for my Union Jacks –
this may be cotton or even denim – and fray the edges so it has
a 'shabby chic' look. Here, I'll show you how to make a flanged
cover (see page 28) – and there's no hand sewing involved.
Of course, you can adapt the design and make an envelope or
hand-finished cushion cover if you prefer.

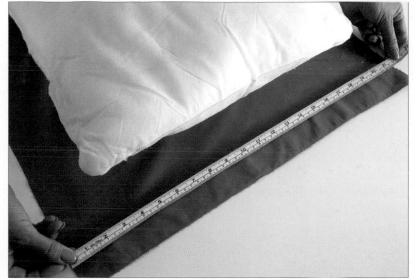

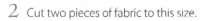

1 Measure your cushion and add an extra 10cm (4in) all around -for the flange.

2 Cut two pieces of fabric to this size.

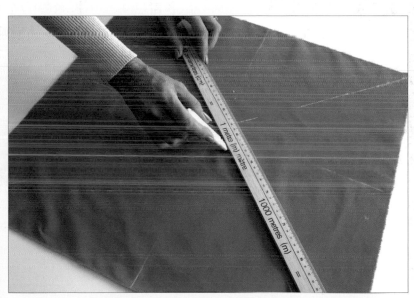

3 Fold one piece (the cushion front) in half and mark the centre line using chalk, then do the same in the other direction. Draw in the diagonals too.

4 Now cut the strips of fabric for the Union Jack design. You will need eight strips all together, in four contrasting fabrics:

Fabric 1: one strip about 8cm (3¼in) wide by the cushion length and one strip about 8cm (3¼in) wide by the cushion width.

Fabric 2: one strip about 4cm (1½in) wide by the cushion length and one strip about 4cm (1½in) wide by the cushion width.

Fabric 3: two strips about 8cm (3¼in) wide by the length of the diagonal.

Fabric 4: two strips about 3cm (1¼in) wide by the length of the diagonal.

Fray the strips a little on each edge.

5 Start with the diagonals. Cut the wider diagonals (fabric 3) in half widthways, spray them with a temporary fabric glue and place them on the cushion cover front.

6 Cut the 3cm (1¼in) widths (fabric 4) in half widthways, spray and glue them over the four pieces you've just placed on the cover. Position them nearer one long edge than the other, as shown in the picture.

7 Stitch the edges of the cross at this point. You can use either straight, zig-zag or embroidery stitches. Then turn the fabric over and snip off the excess.

8 Spray and glue the two remaining 8cm (3¼in) widths (fabric 1) over the centre lines, this time from top to bottom and side to side.

9 Do the same with the 4cm (1½in) widths (fabric 2), laying them centrally over the wider lengths.

10 Stitch the edges of these strips as you did in step 7 and snip off the excess.

11 Sew together three sides of the cushion cover, wrong sides facing, then insert the cushion pad.

12 Carefully push the remaining side under your sewing machine and stitch it closed.

13 Pull at any loose threads to encourage fraying.

Glossary

Basting: temporary stitches to keep pieces of fabric together. These are usually hand-sewn lines of stitching, made with a running stitch about 1cm (½in) in length.

Bias: If something is cut on the true bias, it is cut at 45° to the selvage. On bias binding used for cording, the diagonal cut helps to stop fraying. You can make your own or buy plain binding from fabric stores.

Calico: a closely woven cotton fabric that is used for many crafts. It is a natural cream-coloured cotton, and frequently has cotton seed husk still in it. It comes in a variety of different weights.

Dressmaking shears: choose a good quality scissor as the cut will be more accurate. Dressmaking shears have an angled handle so that the whole of the blade is flat against your fabric. This makes it easier to cut long lengths and straight lines.

Pinking shears: scissors with a saw-tooth edge that leave a zig-zag cut. This helps to stop fraying on woven fabric and makes an interesting pattern on felt.

Raw edge: the cut edge of a piece of fabric. It may fray or unravel if left in this state, but on cushions like the Union Jack (page 91) this is a good look!

eam allowance: the distance from the raw edge to the stitch line, usually 1–1.5cm (½–⅝in) in cushion covers.

Selvage: the woven edge of the fabric, where the weft threads bend around to go in the other direction. Use this as a guide to getting a straight line.

Tacking: the same as basting – temporary stitches that are removed after sewing, or to hold something in place during construction. They are usually removed before the cushion cover is finished, though some may end up hidden inside the cover and may not need to be removed.

Tea: a hot drink you deserve when you've finished your cushion cover!

Childhood keepsakes

Children's clothes fit beautifully on the front of a cushion cover – and what better way to display them! These delightful cushions will bring back happy memories for many years to come. The instructions for making them are provided on pages 84–85.

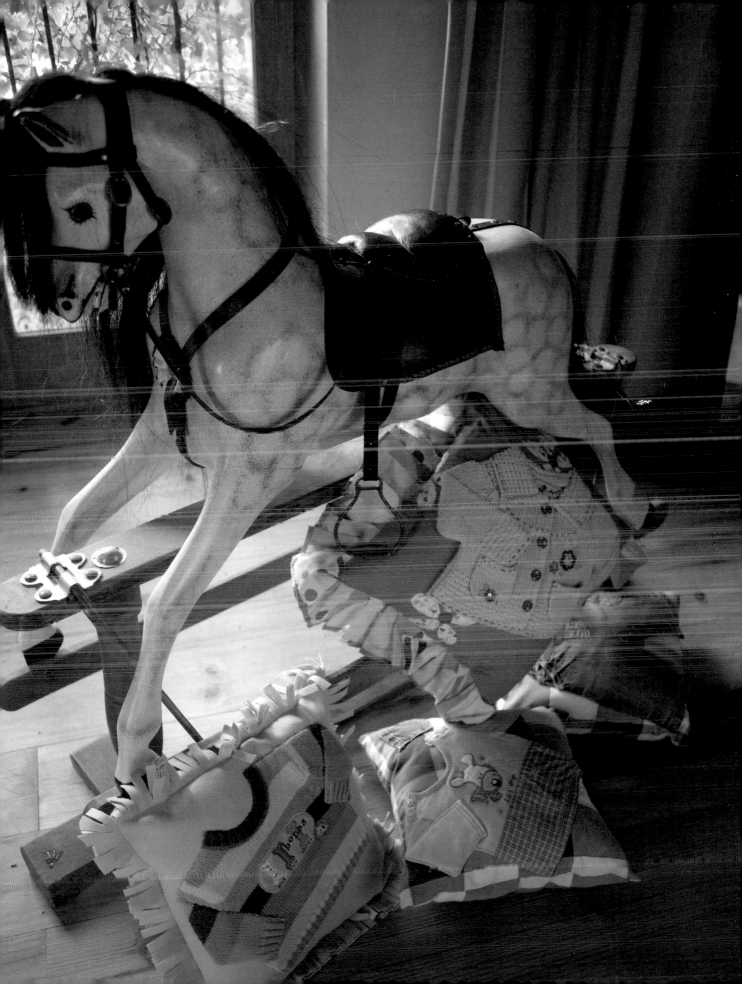

Index